By
Rashad A Young

Copyright © 2023 Rashad A Young
All rights reserved.
ISBN: 9798862097436

DEDICATION

To anyone with a dream, never lose it.

TABLE OF CONTENTS

Acknowledgements I

1 - Nothingness 1

2 - The Journey 10

3 - Live For You 23

4 - Forgiveness 40

5 - Find Your Focus 50

About The Author 57

ACKNOWLEDGEMENTS

I am grateful to God for granting me the ability to be creative and express myself. To my family and friends, I would like to express my gratitude for your support and kindness throughout the entire process of writing this book. To my brother Caleb, thank you for being a part of the audiobook process. I appreciate your strong voice presence as you captivated my words for others to hear. For the rest of you who decide to find some sense of pride and information reading this, I appreciate you for helping me understand myself better.

Much love.

A Wise Word

Promises to turn into forge moments.
Love turns into burning dust.
Old wounds break our hearts.
We can't make it up anymore.

I was once told
Enjoy life what for it is.
Being remorseful is empty
Life is meant to be experienced.
Everyone can't go with you

Forgive yourself
All decisions create opportunities.
Experiencing life is a reminder
That you are alive
You are here
You can build again

Never forget who you are
Love whoever loves you
Try your best
And let the world handle the rest.

1.
NOTHINGNESS

Life is a complex and wondrous phenomenon that has puzzled and fascinated humans for thousands of years. Each new generation that embarks on this human experience comes down to asking the same questions. What are meant to do? What is our purpose? Why am I here? Will I be successful? Will I find love? Will I truly enjoy my life experience? Will I have any regrets in life? Wherever you may land on the spectrum of thought in your life, I hope my book provides a perspective that I am glad I discovered in my twenty-eight years of life. You want to know what it is? Just live your life and stop trying to figure out everything.

Too many of us live with the notion that we have to be perfect or have a certain amount of notoriety to feel better about ourselves. Some feel the need to be successful and drive a Bugatti by thirty and

Renew

believe that if we do not have those things then we are failures. Or that if we are not married or do not have children by a certain age will won't find love. All of it is mundane and wasteful thinking. While people have a right to desire and promote whatever they want in their life, if your life ended today would it matter? I am going to say it again, so it pierces through each of your eyes and ears reading or listening to this book via audiobook; we are all going to die. It does not matter if you're fifty, sixty, seventy, our destination will end the same. So, with that life fact, how should we spend our lives? What is it that is truly important for us?

Life is a journey full of ups and downs, joy and sorrow, love and loss, and ending in death. At its core, life is a precious gift that we should cherish and make the most of. Life is a journey of self-discovery and finding meaning in serving others and serving ourselves to become our highest self. As we navigate the twists and turns of life, we learn about ourselves and our place in the world. We discover our strengths and weaknesses, our passions and fears. We develop our own unique perspectives and worldviews, shaped by our experiences, beliefs, and values. More importantly, we value the concept of self-love, forgiveness, and serving others.

The Happiness Pursuit

Have you ever thought about the number of times in our lives where we wanted to be happy and experience happiness? What exactly is happiness to any of us? Our pursuit of happiness is a driving force in life. However, many of the things we believe will bring us happiness such as material possessions, external validation, or superficial achievements often fall short of fulfilling their promises. True contentment and fulfillment arise from cultivating deep connections, nurturing personal well-being, and aligning our actions with our core values. We are social creatures, wired for connection and community. We form bonds with family, friends, and loved ones, and we seek out meaningful relationships that enrich our lives. We connect with the wider world, with nature, with art, with ideas and knowledge, and with something greater than ourselves.

Renew

It is in these moments of struggle that we often find our greatest growth and transformation. My goal here in this book is not to promote a monolithic way of thinking. It is to create an understanding of recognizing the power we have in our lives comes from the understanding of the life that we live. Fixation, procrastination, and idolization are conduits to making our lives lose meaning. We are meant to continuously create to find more within ourselves. When I say create that is based on your strengths and things that bring you joy in your life. When it comes to happiness you must remember that chasing happiness cannot be the goal in life. Obtaining and maintaining peace is what is more important. To chase is to consistently pull and tug to obtain a reward. The problem is, to chase is to continue to overcome. Happiness is like any other emotion; it is temporary and your viewpoint when it comes to happiness will change as we become older. What makes us happy now may look different in ten years.

Embracing this truth and understanding that most things in life are simple liberates us from the burdens of trivial concerns and allows us to focus

Renew

on what genuinely enriches our lives. By redirecting our attention towards the significant aspects of our existence, we can cultivate a sense of purpose, find deeper meaning, and lead a more fulfilling life. Letting go of the insignificant allows us to embrace the profound, fostering meaningful relationships and more importantly being content with our human experience.

Perhaps the most profound aspect of life is its impermanence. We are all mortal beings with a finite amount of time on this earth. This realization can be daunting, but it can also be a powerful motivator to live our lives to the fullest. We can choose to make each moment count, to savor the beauty of the world around us, to love fiercely, and to pursue our dreams with passion and purpose. If we took a second to recognize the amount of power that our minds and thoughts have in our everyday lives, we would operate much differently. Every waking second of our lives we can find ourselves worrying about things we cannot control. That control takes away the power of who we truly are.

Renew

Rather it is spent relentlessly on occupations that will continue beyond our existence. Siting in meetings is pointless because what we truly want to do looks much different than our current positions and careers. Worrying about obtaining more money for "freedom" or just enough to scrape by. Or fixating on relationships and friendships that do not serve us anymore. Focusing on television shows and watching that new episode at everyone is talking about. Scrolling through social media, attempting to find the latest thing to gossip about in our group chat about who is dating who or what insane policies the latest unhinged politician is pushing to mandate. Or who is getting their fifteen minutes of fame from a viral video. I am not knocking those who indulge in those things because we all do and sometimes it can help us escape from the toughness of life and find enjoyment. When you truly think about it, does any of that matter? At your deepest core, you realize none of it matters and it is temporary to our actual human experience. When I began writing this book, this question dawned on me: What would you do if today was your last day on earth? Think about that. What would you do?

Renew

Fading Light Thoughts

The light for our lives will fade at some point. Thinking about one's mortality is something that requires a level of understanding, but once it is recognized and accepted, it is the first step to living a fulfilling life. It is that outside of this question alone, most of us will be unable to answer that question because we live in ignorance that we will wake up tomorrow and our lives will remain the same. It is how we are conditioned to think. Think about how many times you have told someone you will see them tomorrow. Or talk about plans for your upcoming weekend. This life is what we know.

We do not know what life is like when we die. We have no idea of what our next destination will look like. It is easy to be caught in the cycle of repetitive actions. The moment you realize that our cycle of living needs to be broken the freer you will become. Is life meant to be like this? No, it is meant to be enjoyed for what it is. Being in the moment, enjoying time with our loved ones, and more importantly, finding happiness in ourselves and the people celebrating our existence. What was the

Renew

meaning of this section? Nothing absolutely nothing. That is how life should be sometimes and being present and enjoying the moment for what it is.

We all start somewhere.

2.
THE JOURNEY

Peace and blessings to you all. Thank you for deciding to pick up my second book in my self-development installment series, titled *Renew*. If you are here picking up this book today rather physically or via audiobook, I truly thank you for taking the time to read or listen. I say humbly as a writer it is always a dream of mine to provide value in hopes to create something meaningful. With books, I can sit here and create some false promise that this book will change your life.

I would be remiss to have that notion of thinking. Any information can change our life and while I would hope this is the book that would do that, I know in the same light that this book may not do anything for you and that is okay. I believe the information we share with others is tied with our personal experiences, energy and intentions and

Renew

with this these are pure exchanges of energy. I believe the things we think or say hold true power and you are here for something; I wrote this for something, and I am forever grateful for each of you embarking on this experience with me. Life is about expressing art. I consider myself an artist, not an author. I use books as a form of expression in the hopes that you find your own meaning behind them. I genuinely believe that everything we do, or experience has a deeper meaning behind it. For you, this book may shift your thinking. This book may give you the spark you need to challenge yourself for the better. Or it may do nothing at all and become a coffee coaster in your living room. Either way, I did not write this with the notion that I can sell you a product without the purpose of wanting your dollar alone. I wanted to give you my version of art for the world to share.

I believe in universal truths and simplicity in my work. I feel this book was guided for me to write. In fact, this book tugged at my heart for a long time. Between my first book, *Be Formless*, and where I stand today, I am nowhere near the same person that I was five years ago. I sometimes cringe at my first

Renew

book because of how much my ideals and thoughts have shifted and evolved. I have experienced more. I have made more mistakes and learned more lessons. Through it all I came to the realization that my ability to share these lessons instead of gatekeeping my experience for myself is doing the world a disservice. Each of us has a story worth mentioning. It does not matter how many followers we have or how much money we obtain; each of us can learn something from one another. I hope that this book provides you with a feeling of peace and love. More importantly a sense of purpose in knowing that wherever you may stand in life today you can change.

One of the inspirations behind this book is knowing that I needed to change. I needed to become better as a person. Change is something that many of us desire but fail to realize the truth behind it; Change requires discomfort. Change starts with you, and you are here to take charge of the things you can control and start anew. We have the power to change but we enjoy being comfortable with knowing where we are today. Whomever wants to change must know that changing for the better should be our ultimate goal.

Fear

When I decided to write this book, I must admit two things. First, I was afraid to write this. I found myself in a state of confusion, comparison, and doubt. I am a person that lives in their head often and because of that, my fear turned into procrastination and procrastination is one of our biggest detriments as individuals. It is because of our ability to procrastinate and live in comfort that we can forget the beauty of the gifts and skills we possess as individuals. One of our greatest strengths in life is recognizing our potential and coming in truth with our true self. When experiencing such a power in our lives we often can find ourselves more fearful of who we can become instead of what we can become.

Think about it, people alone can influence our abilities, self-love, gifts, and thoughts. Imagine what we can do as people to hinder ourselves? One of our human flaws is our inability to get out of our own way. We find ways to hinder our growth instead of stepping into the freedom of opportunities. This book needed to be free from my mind and heart. I realized I needed to run towards the fear instead of running away from it. When I started to think beyond myself that is when the realization of why this book needed to be written started to outweigh the reasons why I was afraid to write this. Fear is a natural and necessary part of our survival. It has played a crucial role in keeping our ancestors safe by alerting them to potential risks and triggering the fight-or-flight response. When faced with a genuine threat, fear mobilizes our bodies, heightens our senses, and prepares us to act. It is an instinct that has been honed over millennia of evolution, allowing us to navigate dangerous situations and protect ourselves from harm.

Moreover, fear can serve as a valuable teacher. It can illuminate our vulnerabilities, highlighting areas where we need to be cautious and vigilant. Fear prompts us to evaluate potential risks and make informed decisions. By recognizing and respecting our fears, we can develop strategies to mitigate them and ensure our safety. In this sense, fear acts as a wise counselor, urging us to tread carefully and take necessary precautions. Fear has the power to paralyze us, preventing us from pursuing our goals, embracing new experiences, and reaching our full potential. Fear can create self-doubt, feed on insecurities, and reinforce negative thought patterns. It can erect barriers that prevent us from exploring uncharted territories, whether they be physical, intellectual, or emotional. By succumbing to fear, we may find ourselves trapped in a cycle of stagnation, unable to break free and evolve. To confront the truth of fear, it is crucial to recognize the distinction between rational and irrational fears.

Rational fears are based on genuine threats or risks, such as fear of physical harm or danger. These fears warrant attention and should be addressed with care. Irrational fears, on the other hand, are often unfounded and rooted in distorted perceptions or past experiences. Facing our fears requires courage and resilience. It involves acknowledging and accepting them, rather than suppressing or denying them. It means stepping out of our comfort zones and embracing uncertainty. By gradually exposing ourselves to our fears, we can build resilience and develop a greater sense of self-confidence. By understanding the role of fear and differentiating between rational and irrational fears, we can cultivate a healthier relationship with this innate human emotion. By facing our fears head-on, we can transcend our limitations, unlock our potential, and embark on a journey of personal growth and self-discovery.

Embracing Transformation

The other side of the turmoil of this book was the creation of this book was written during a fearful time of my life. I experienced an extreme transformation. Our lives never go as planned. The people we believe will be in our lives forever end up being a simple moment in time. Transformation can come from both good and bad experiences. What causes an experience to be good or bad is how you view it. I am sure we know the saying "if you want God to laugh at you tell him your plans." It is a reminder that things happen in life and because of that all we can do is embrace it. Nonetheless, that is the beauty of life when it comes to experiencing the

Renew

unknown. Embracing transformation can be a powerful tool for personal growth and development. Transformation involves letting go of old patterns or beliefs that no longer serve us, and embracing new ones that align with our goals and values.

One way to embrace transformation is to cultivate a growth mindset. This involves viewing challenges and failures as opportunities for learning and growth, rather than as setbacks. When we have a growth mindset, we are more likely to take risks, try new things, and persist in the face of obstacles. Another way to embrace transformation is to practice self-reflection. This involves taking the time to reflect on our thoughts, feelings, and behaviors, and to identify areas where we would like to make changes. Self-reflection can help us to gain clarity about our goals and values, and to develop a plan for achieving them

For a long time, I did not recognize the true power I had within myself because of my pride in wanting to share with others. Yet alone, take the time to be honest with myself on how I can improve as an individual and a man. Pride can be our biggest

Renew

determinant as people. Our pride can ruin many blessings and opportunities for us but, the moment you get out of your own way is the moment you can begin to find peace in your life. During my transformation, I realized I needed to accept where I was in life and begin to take the steps towards the person I desire to become. I had to shift my mindset and realize that I could be experiencing this time alone but, I am surrounded by people who love me dearly. More importantly, take this moment of transformation and isolation to understand the beauty of loving myself for who I am and what I bring to the world. In our darkest times is where our light can begin to expand.

The reason I am sharing this is to let you know that sometimes in life we go through difficult times, and it is okay. You can still find peace in a world that sometimes may not appear so peaceful. You can create your own paradise no matter where you are. It starts with your attitude and the way you view things. Your life and environment are both products of your thoughts and actions. That is not to say that if you think of these things you will forget about your reality. That is the real challenge.

Renew

Detachment

Detaching yourself from the outcome of your current experience to your future experience. Once you detach you can begin to attract whatever it is your heart and mind desires, especially if it is meant for you. You have the power to take charge of your life and create the world you desire. The moment you realize your own power is the moment you can truly change your life. I will preface that changing your life does not happen drastically. It does not shift as soon as you want it to shift. You will experience the hard times, breakdowns, and days you want to give up. However, the is the beauty of the journey. Pain is designed to be a reminder that no matter what you are experiencing you are stronger and are prepared to endure more for the better. Life indeed happens for you and not to you. Each of us will experience an unfathomable amount of pain and hurt in our lives. The root of humanity is found through our suffering. However, suffering creates peace as you move forward.

Renew

The Purpose Of Renew

Renew is a book designed to help you reshape your life no matter the situation that you're in. One beauty about life is that we can push past the things that we encounter. If we allow life to dictate our actions, we will live a life full of regret and resentment. Truthfully, nobody wants to live that way. We want to live free and be free from the obstructive nature that society places among us.

We should be free to be who we are, believe what we believe, and love who we want to love. Nobody knows what happens after we leave this human experience and focusing on judging how someone else operates is the quickest way to never be fulfilled. This book is meant to be quick, consider it a reference point in your journey of life. I do not have a million dollars to give you. I cannot tell you how to succeed in your business or relationship but, I can tell you what I believe is crucial to your level of success in your life. Our external successes only get us so far and while generational wealth is the key for most of us alive today, the truth is that generational wealth will be

Renew

here when you transition. Focusing on your experience and how you live is most important. The money will come if you stay strategic, focus on your craft, serve others and love yourself purely. What is true is that many people die trying to live instead of living until you die.

That is the difference we find ourselves purging our emotional well-being into things that if it was our last day on earth won't hold any value to our lives. It is not to say to live life without ambitions and goals. No please strive for all things you want in life. However, consider this book as a reminder to focus on living the life you truly desire. I believe to renew yourself physically, mentally, and spiritually, there are three rules to live by.

1. Live for you
2. Forgive
3. Find your focus

Renew

With these three things, I believe if you apply these concepts in your life, you will become as free as you can be. Is it easy? Absolutely not. Nothing in life is easy. You should do it shared and with an open heart and a pure spirit. Take this as a reminder that your journey is your journey. Be who you are meant to be and do the things you are designed to do in the world.

3.
LIVE FOR YOU

What does it mean to live for you? Living for oneself means prioritizing one's own needs, desires, values, and well-being in the choices and actions taken in life. It is about seeking personal fulfillment, happiness, and self-actualization while considering one's interests and aspirations as paramount. It means making decisions based on personal values, passions, and goals rather than succumbing to external pressures or societal expectations. It requires authenticity and self-awareness, as individuals who live for themselves strive to align their actions with their true selves, rather than conforming to others' expectations or conforming to societal norms that do not resonate with them. In life, you must be inherently selfish when it comes to defining the life that you want yourself. You must be selfish with yourself to know how to best serve yourself.

Renew

The concept of self-love and self-awareness while most of us hear or talk about it truly lacks the understanding of the power and nature of the power behind it. Our external desires are often latched from the idea of the perspective of others and the need to be approved. Think about it, what would the world truly be like if we lived through the lens of status or ego? Who would people idolize? Who would be jealous or envious? Who would be considered the top of the top? Who would be considered "relationship goals?" That is how our society has created a new monster in our lives. Instead of life making us understand the beauty and value we bring to ourselves we find ourselves comparing, worrying, judging, and criticizing others to make ourselves feel better. It is a difference between being selfish in life and being selfish for the type of life you want. Here's the thing, you cannot live for others until you know what it means to live for you.

Outside of our external aspirations we have an internal flame this needs to grow and be fed. To succeed with self, you must be selfish in ways that make you progress to becoming a better person. No

Renew

matter what your goals, desires, or dreams are; you are responsible for them. I know often we think about the concept of being selfish as a concept as being negative yet, it is a truth that you must think about yourself first before you can be of service to someone else. You must constantly desire a need for change and improvement.

To be selfish is to analyze and live in a space of awareness. No one wants to appear selfish. It is a word that is often associated with greed, power, and the abuse of others. However, there are many ways in which being selfish can be a good thing. To be selfish is creating an understanding that you cannot operate optimally without making sure you are good first. That means taking care of your health and well-being. Sometimes people neglect their health, mental, and emotional wellbeing because they are worried about how those around them feel or if they are making everyone else happy. A big misconception that occurs in relationships, partnerships, or friendships is that we find ourselves pouring more into others than we do ourselves. It is natural because we want the people, we love to feel loved but, there's a time and place for things of that nature. If you have the capacity to do more for others, then do more for others.

Giving is a natural thing many of us will do when it comes to the people that we love. It becomes self-sacrificing when you endure more than you can handle for others who are not pouring into you the same way. You must be okay with yourself rather people stay in your life or leave. The reality is that people will come and go. It is natural for us as people to feel attached to people, relationships, possessions, and other external items that have us emotionally tugged and struggling making yourself better. However, for the greater good of yourself you must remember to put that same energy, love, and commitment into you.

Isolation

"Who truly wants to be alone?" I remember asking my therapist that question during one of my therapy sessions. My reasoning for this question wasn't about being alone due to a lack of a relationship, it was based on the notion of experiencing periods of life alone. Some of us struggle with doing anything alone. Think about it, when's the last time you truly enjoyed your own company? When was the last time you took the time to learn more about yourself and ways to improve yourself?

Isolation is a period in our lives that all of us need to experience. To sit in a moment of solace and check us find new ways to improve ourselves There is a truth that many of us must understand early; you must be okay with being yourself and whatever that looks like. Your healing journey begins when you are open to reliving your experience to open your emotions fully. However, the key to living for yourself first is healing your inner child.

Healing Your Inner Child

Healing your inner child refers to the process of addressing and healing emotional wounds that originated in childhood. These emotional wounds can be caused by various factors such as trauma, neglect, or a lack of emotional support. The inner child represents the vulnerable, emotional part of us that was formed during childhood. When our emotional needs were not met, or we experienced

Renew

trauma or difficult experiences, our inner child may have been wounded. These wounds can manifest in various ways, such as low self-esteem, fear of abandonment, or difficulty forming healthy relationships.

To heal your inner child, it is important to acknowledge and validate the emotional pain and trauma that you experienced as a child. This can involve connecting with your inner child through visualization or other therapeutic techniques, and providing them with the love, support, and validation they needed but did not receive. It may also involve examining the beliefs and patterns that were formed because of childhood experiences and challenging those that no longer serve you. For example, if you were constantly criticized as a child, you may have developed a belief that you are not good enough.

By recognizing and challenging this belief, you can begin to reframe your self-image in a more positive light. Healing your inner child can be a difficult and ongoing process, but it can also be incredibly rewarding. By addressing the emotional

Renew

wounds of the past, you can create a foundation for greater emotional resilience, self-esteem, and overall well-being. One of the biggest gifts that has come into my life is the gift of therapy. I will admit that prior to my journey to therapy I was skeptical about the power of it. Like most men in particular black men, we often can view vulnerability as a weakness. Our viewing of vulnerability is passed down through other men, society, and sometimes women. This idea of being a shell of themselves; almost robotic state of living is one of the most damaging things that we could ever experience, and we unfortunately do not understand the magnitude of living as damaged creatures.

As I have reflected on my life and the way I handled myself in many situations I have learned that this new open and healed version of myself would be ashamed of my previous self because of the hurt I have caused upon others due to my inability to be open emotionally. If you can go to a therapist, I recommend it. It will truly change your life if done properly. That means being honest with yourself and understanding that your healing journey will not succeed overnight. In fact, I believe

Renew

as you do the work you will find yourself in a state of regression sometimes more than you feel you are progressing. That just means you are working towards the right path of becoming your pure self again. You should unlearn things about yourself and what others have taught you to relearn and improve.

Battle Scars and Vices

Many of us have lived a life where we have been on a battlefield. A battlefield of pain, suffering, trials and tribulations. The thing is many of us do not realize that we have been on this battlefield our entire life. You started to become a member of this battlefield when you were a child. You were innocent, creative, and filled with love. At some point, you received your first bruise. Now this bruise could have come from experiencing extreme trauma, or simply having your feelings hurt by someone you love or trust such as your parent or close friend. Either way you realize that life has some pain to it. It is not as pleasant and safe as we believe it is.

Renew

We must remember that our battlefield, this war that we experience occurs in two places. The first place is our external or the things we see. These experiences are more instant; we can respond to the damage instantly. While it is still painful, as a child these bruises can potentially be patched up by our loved ones to remind us of everything will be okay. It is like that time you fell off your bike and scraped your knee. You put some peroxide or alcohol on it; it stung for a moment, and you got back up. That is how many of us deal with the external battle. We take the pain and get back up.

The other battle is the war in your mind. Now this battle can ruin your entire existence before you truly get a chance to live. This is where I suffered for a long time in my life as someone who lives in their head. This is where all the memories, both good and bad, store in your mind and soul for years. After you get a few bruises, you start finding ways to protect yourself from future bruises because you do not feel safe enough exposing yourself for who you truly are. Vulnerability is our greatest strength and detriment if people or situations do not protect our true essence with the same pure intentions that

Renew

we have with being open. Maybe you become more closed off when these things happen. You become less trusting of yourself. Now this is where the mind battle gets trickier.

You begin to discover that you can find ways to eliminate this pain through a vice. These vices could come in the form of food, pleasure, entertainment, or any other form of escapism. The problem is though once you open the door to one vice more vices can begin to enter your world. I believe in transparency and for you to understand my world I will share with you, my voice. My personal vice was self-pleasure. It was the safest for me to hide my pain from the world and not something as noticeable that could affect my appearance such as drinking, drugs, or excessive eating. Now, I will admit that my experience is my experience, and I will never tell you that exploring these vices will ruin your life simply by exploring them. The real issue becomes when you start to become dependent on them unconsciously. When I started to feel down about myself, stressed, confused, or wanted to feel in control of my life.

Renew

While it has been months since I have gone down that road, I recognize through reflection that my wounds from childhood created a portal to the door of this vice. My feelings of worthlessness, fear, and wanting to please others too much made me enter this dark path. I thank God, I freed myself from that path because it was truly ruining my life. While it wasn't an everyday thing for me, I often found myself going through binge moments to block any pain I was experiencing and truthfully as I found myself working through my issues in therapy, the binging got worse. Again, this was my vice because I was able to conceal my struggles without others knowing. I often lived through a lens of people finding value in their lives and often it can be assumed that I have things all together. I wanted to keep this "perfect" image intact selfishly so people wouldn't judge me for being something different than how I presented myself.

Once you realize you are performing for others you will easily discover the cracks in yourself that will cause your dam to break over. However, I realized to change my life and be the person I know I am designed and capable of being I had to deal

Renew

with my wounds head on. I wanted to be a person that was his inner child again. I wanted to love freely and give someone and myself that same level of purity we once all experienced before as children. Your inner child is the source of living the life as pure as you can. Your inner child is pure and filled with love. At some point, that inner child became damaged and wounded. It became a shell of itself to protect itself from the monsters under the bed. To free your inner child from its protective shell, practice acceptance and unconditional love. Each of us as children was given certain skills and characteristics that naturally define us for who we are. It could have been your ability to process information quickly, draw, write, athletics, business, cook, make music, debate, or serve others. Within each of our natural skills and abilities, we were visionaries on that dream or goal.

At some point in life that dream is in the process of becoming a reality or has become derailed. However, the inner desire within you knows that when you are in that natural space of your skill or ability you feel as if you are at home. Why is that? It is because you know at your core that is

Renew

something that your inner child will hold on to forever. When you think about living for you remind yourself what would your inner child say about this situation or experience? Ask yourself, "What do I need right now?" Talk to yourself with a compassionate voice as if you would talk to a dear friend. Explore any blockages that come up and express them in healthy ways. Write down your feelings in a journal, take a creative art class, practice breathing exercises, dance, get outside into nature or seek out a therapist.

When I started to formulate this book, I was in a state of deep reflection. I thought about my life and the experiences I have faced that lead me to my personal healing journey. Each traumatic or negative experience chained my inner child up even more causing me to become more of a shell of myself. When you decide that you have had enough of experiencing the pain, depression, anxiety, anger, and sadness you will do anything to make yourself feel like a child again.

Renew

Ego

Our inner struggle with ego is a matter of learning how to master our thoughts and conquer our negative emotions, and then to be our authentic, creative selves. As you become used to remaining in the truth of your highest self, the false ego-self will dissipate itself. If you are looking for happiness, find it in your true self, not the illusion of this world that the ego keeps offering to keep you stuck in your ego. At some point, you must realize the false sense of self-worth that you gain by sticking to your guns and being right does not trump real happiness. Just like you can train your mind to be more forgiving and self-aware, you can train your mind to be satisfied with what you have. Understanding your true self and practicing self-awareness helps you realize you cannot be right every time. Get out of your own way; acknowledge the harm that your ego, left unchecked, can do; and start winning.

Your ego needs to struggle and protect itself. Your ego needs negative situations to occur for it to have things to do, things to worry about, or things to change. Our ego - insistent - may show up as a gesture, look, a word, or action, but the result is usually the same. Being mindful of the demands our ego makes, recognizing the signs it makes, offers ways of dealing with it, and finds ways of fighting or keeping it under control. Once we acknowledge that our resolute self or ego is a grave danger to our best efforts--that our lives and efforts in this world, and our progress in the next, are dependent upon the decisions we make--we recognize the need for vigilance. Our egos -- insistent, grasping, demanding lower selves within us all -- can cause the elation of life to vanish in a moment.

Soon enough, your ego-self would know these people, and you would find out they were not as happy as they seemed.

Self-Love

We often overlook the importance of loving ourselves first to create a happy and fulfilling life. Unfortunately, self-love can be one of the hardest things to practice, especially in today's fast-paced

Renew

world. But it is critical that we make self-care and self-love a priority in our lives. Self-love is an essential component of living a healthy and fulfilling life. When we prioritize our own needs and self-care, we become stronger, more confident, and happier. Taking care of ourselves and loving ourselves unconditionally helps us to build healthier relationships with others and lead more meaningful lives.

For me and my battle with self, I am always finding a way to find logic in any situation. The problem with that is that I try to find answers now in time where an answer or solution cannot be found. It is like someone who prays to God, universe, or the source and want an answer immediately. We find ourselves asking for our desires in a way that is shown loudly and vividly. We want a sign to make us convinced that we are not crazy. When we do not get the things, we want the way we want them, we find ourselves in a state of suffering and chasing the need of wanting to remove the feeling of nothingness. Our desires can be our biggest blessings and demise. It is our inability to have faith and lead our own

Renew

understanding that can make us forget how powerful it is to ensure that regardless of what happens we will be fine. Living for yourself means that you accept who you are and love yourself for it. It means that you can identify and meet your own needs without feeling guilty or ashamed.

Living for yourself means making decisions that are best for you and will lead to a life of fulfillment. It is not about selfishness but rather understanding that your needs come first. If your decisions are based on taking care of yourself, chances are you will be successful in whatever path you choose to take. Whatever you do to embark on your journey with self, please give yourself grace and understanding. Nobody is perfect and even in our flaws we are beautiful individuals inside and out.

4.
FORGIVENESS

I will admit writing this chapter was a struggle in a joking way yet true. We can say that we forgive people but truthfully, we hold on to the past grudges with individuals often more than we what to admit. In my time doing inner work and attempting to better myself, I have learned that forgiveness is more than just about forgiving someone and their actions. It is about forgiving yourself for the various experiences you have faced in your life. Rather that is with people, jobs, or other outside influences you have endured.

I can assure you that if you apply this method to your life, you will see a dramatic shift in your life immediately. The purest way to love anything in this word is to forgive. We all hurt one another in some shape of form and because one's action can determine the process of which forgiveness occurs

Renew

and how quickly it occurs. It is often said that forgiveness is a process, and there are many steps along the way. What does it mean to forgive? How many of us can truly say we forgive others? What is true is that in life when we connect with others no matter the level of the relationship or connection with someone there is a level of trust and care we expect to have in that experience. When that trust or respect is broken, it can lead us to experience holding grudges or resentment.

Forgiveness is a personal journey, and the time and process required to forgive may vary from person to person. It is not always easy and may involve facing and working through complex emotions. To forgive means to let go of feelings of resentment, anger, or the desire for revenge toward someone who has caused harm, hurt, or offense. It involves releasing negative emotions and choosing to relinquish the need for retaliation or holding a grudge. It does not necessarily mean forgetting the offense or condoning the actions. Rather, forgiveness is a personal act of liberation, freeing oneself from the burden of carrying negative

Renew

emotions and allowing for emotional healing and growth.

One of the most important steps is forgiving yourself. It can be difficult to forgive others if you are unable to first forgive yourself. Forgiving yourself is essential to self-growth and personal development. It allows us to take responsibility for our mistakes and learn from them, rather than harboring feelings of resentment or shame. It gives us a chance to show ourselves kindness, understanding, and compassion. We all make mistakes in life, but it is important not to dwell on those mistakes. Instead, forgive yourself and move on. When we forgive ourselves, we can let go of the guilt and regret associated with our past wrongdoings and focus instead on the lessons we've learned from them.

This also helps us become more mindful and aware of our actions, which can lead to better decision-making and fewer mistakes in the future. Additionally, forgiving can reduce stress, anxiety, and even physical ailments related to holding onto unresolved emotions. By recognizing our

Renew

shortcomings, forgiving ourselves for our mistakes, and understanding that everyone makes mistakes, we can begin to take more positive steps toward self-improvement and personal growth.

Everything and everyone we encounter is a form of energy and most of us carry that energy around twenty-four seven. The moment you realize that you are not your past or the experiences your past may have presented you with is the moment you realize you control your energy. This energy influences who we are and how we move in this life. You ever notice that as a child we live through life effortlessly and with purity? Once we start receiving harmful energy in our lives from our families, friends, or society itself, it starts to shape and molds us into who we are today.

If you are not learning about or practicing aspects of forgiveness, you often beat yourself up and will have trouble moving past mistakes. When you accept that you are not perfect, you will not find it so difficult to forgive yourself for mistakes. When you find yourself having a hard time forgiving yourself, this can cause emotional,

Renew

mental, and physical damage. Guilt and regret are both highly powerful emotions, representing feelings of hurt, which can result in self-punishment. You had the narrative in your head that you were wrong, and now you are telling them you feel this way. Even if you apologized to those you have hurt, and started the process of forgiving yourself, you are still probably going to feel awkward about your actions - if only because you are still worried about what others are going to think about you.

If you want to forgive yourself, you need to begin by identifying the concrete hurts, the regrets, mistakes, and decisions you are carrying around. Whether you are trying to move past a small error or one that impacts every aspect of your life, the steps you should take to forgive yourself will be similar. Learning forgiveness is all about freeing yourself from guilt and shame related to the situation that hurt you. Learn how guilt and shame hold us back, why beating ourselves up can be addicting, and how to forgive yourself we examine how regret can catalyze change, what holds us back from self-forgiveness, and how to reconcile with your past mistakes - and move on to better things. Reminding ourselves that we did our best with the tools and knowledge available to us at that moment helps us forgive and move on.

Learning how to work through feelings of guilt while steering clear of feelings of shame will keep us from responding in ways that we may regret, or worse, continuing to feel awful about what we cannot change. Genuine self-forgiveness helps to re-establish a sense of moral worth and dignity, even when you made a major mistake that caused significant harm to others or to yourself. We can practice compassion toward ourselves each day and expressing self-love.

Live In Truth

Your truth is everything. Speaking your mind and speaking your truth is a crucial aspect to living a passionate, fulfilled, authentic life. Our focus on authenticity is all about discovering the value to yourself and to the people you love - in living a fully authentic life. Loving and living authentically is about understanding the value that you bring, not

Renew

backing down from those who disregard or belittle you. The power of loving your unique being and willing to look in the mirror and recognize your own truth. The fact is fear and resistance can become most apparent when you are living your truth.

To discover this realization, first, you must realize how you have been conditioning yourself to live from society as truth rather than your own. Living a life of secrets and lies, well beyond your own truth, may seem euphoric at first, that is, until it starts messing with your beliefs about what kind of person you want to be in the world. Living in your truth becomes reality the day you choose to take charge of your life, to live the life you want to live, and do the things daily that bring you joy and pleasure. Living in your truth is simply about living your truest self, doing things every day that bring you happiness and joy, living your truest self. Living life honoring your authentic self; doing things that you know you should be doing. Now, I am not saying that you should not have a career, or have kids, or get married, or be a stay-at-home mom - not at all, because there are some people who

Renew

live in their truest selves, who are overjoyed and content in their lives.

When you are unclear on what is our purpose in life, saying yes, all the time is a cheap way to get people to like you. My truth in doing so, however, may be that I am worried you are going to hurt my feelings, or that I dislike some of the things you are doing, and this makes me feel unsafe and uncomfortable around you. I stress yours, and your truth, both, here, because your truth is not going to be like anybody else's truth. Speaking our truths not only frees us, but it also has the potential to change things for others, bringing us closer to them. When we accept our journey, and view it through that lens, there is a chance that a massive change can occur in our lives, that we start attracting to ourselves a greater number of the things that we need & want.

Love Freely

In a world where everything comes with conditions, loving freely can feel like a revolutionary act. But it does not have to be. Loving freely simply means you do not withhold your affection or love based on what someone else has or has not done. You love them just as they are, regardless of their mistakes or shortcomings. True unconditional love comes without conditions or attachments and is given freely without expectation. It is a powerful way to demonstrate forgiveness to the people in your life, no matter how small or large their offense may have been.

Loving freely takes practice, but the rewards are worth it. It teaches us how to open our hearts and embrace our loved ones without judgment or expectations. Practicing this kind of love allows us to accept ourselves for who we are and forgive ourselves for our own mistakes. It also helps us forgive others, understanding that even when we make mistakes, we can still be worthy of love. Love freely and you will be surprised at how much your relationships with others will improve, and how

Renew

much easier it will become to forgive. Remember, no matter what mistakes have been made in the past, true unconditional love never fails. This is a reminder that our greatest strength in life is not to be self-righteous but is to forgive ourselves and others every day. Forgiving does not mean you will forget what a person has done to you.

You simply realize the energy of holding on to what has occurred holds no true value in the core of who you are. Your time is priceless along with your energy. Please protect both at all costs. In the end, forgiveness can bring a sense of liberation, emotional healing, and a renewed ability to experience joy and peace. It empowers individuals to break free from the shackles of resentment and anger, fostering personal growth, and promoting healthier relationships with others and oneself.

5.
FIND YOUR FOCUS

Finding focus in life is an important part of personal growth and well-being. Finding your focus can help you stay on track and help you to achieve your goals and make progress in your life. It is essential to take the time to look inward and discover what matters to you so that you can prioritize and create a plan that works best for you. To start focusing, take a few moments to ask yourself some questions. What do you want to accomplish? What do you need to do to get there? What are the values or beliefs that are important to you and will guide you as you make decisions? Knowing the answers to these questions can give you clarity and help you find the focus you need to move forward.

Once you have identified your goals and priorities, it is important to create a plan that allows you to stay focused. That may mean blocking out time in your schedule for specific tasks or activities, breaking down projects into smaller steps, or setting deadlines for yourself. Staying organized and taking small steps toward your goals can help you keep your focus and make progress. By focusing on your desires and self you will be more productive and motivated as you work towards achieving your goals. Taking a few moments to check in with yourself can go a long way in helping you stay on track and reach your full potential.

Watch Who You Allow In Your Life

"Watch who you allow in your life" is a phrase that highlights the importance of being selective and intentional about the people we choose to spend time with and let into our inner circle. This is because the people we surround ourselves with can have a significant impact on our mental, emotional, and even physical well-being. Negative or toxic people can drain our energy, lower our self-esteem, and even lead us down a destructive path. They may engage in behaviors such as gossip, manipulation,

Renew

or criticism, and may not respect our boundaries or values. On the other hand, positive and supportive people can lift us up, provide encouragement and inspiration, and help us grow and thrive. It is important to be mindful of the energy and vibes that people bring into our lives, and to set boundaries when necessary.

This can involve limiting or ending contact with negative or toxic people, and seeking out relationships with those who share our values and goals. It can also involve being honest and assertive in communicating our needs and boundaries to others. It is important to note that not all relationships are perfect, and conflict and disagreements are a natural part of any relationship. However, it is important to evaluate whether the benefits of a relationship outweigh the costs, and to be mindful of how a person's presence in our lives affects us. It is important to be selective about who you choose to keep in your life. Allowing toxic people into your life can have negative effects on your mental, emotional and physical health. It is essential to establish boundaries when it comes to choosing who you spend your time with. When

Renew

selecting individuals to surround yourself with, ask yourself a few simple questions: Does this person make me feel valued? Do they support my goals and ambitions? Do I feel safe around them? Do I feel a connection to this person? If the answer to any of these questions is no, then it might be wise to reconsider that relationship. It is not always easy to cut ties with people, but for your own sake, sometimes it is necessary. On the other hand, having people in your life that genuinely care about you, respect your values and give you encouragement can be extremely beneficial.

Having positive relationships with people can provide a sense of security and fulfillment, while also helping to boost your self-esteem. So, make sure that you are spending time with people who are good for you and will support you on your journey through life.

One thing to know about people who truly love you is that these people will want what is always best for you without having expectations of their own self-serving pleasures. We can find ourselves in connections and relationships that do not hold a true purpose in our lives. We should work hard to keep them up float and as we should know protecting our energy is important not only for our growth but also for finding our focus. When distractions are around your life you always be distracted.

Internal Happiness

I know we often hear about the concept of having one life, but do we understand the magnitude of that concept. It is important to understand how rare it is right now to be alive as a human being in today's world. The majority of our lives are centered around pleasing and being accepted by others. Since you were a child, someone has provided you with directions on how to live this life. When it comes to life, we only have one shot at it. As individuals, we are here for a limited amount of time. We won't live forever, and we will eventually leave this world as all humans do.

When we come to terms with this concept, we can begin to prioritize what matters most to us. This can include relationships with family, friends, and

Renew

even us. We can learn to focus on our passions and develop new skills that will help us to become the best version of ourselves. Additionally, it can lead us to understand how precious life is and how important it is to forgive others and ourselves when needed. Life can be difficult, but by understanding that we are only here once and that the present moment is a gift, we can learn to move forward in a positive direction and make the most of our lives. It is easy to get caught up in the negativity of life and forget about what truly brings us joy. We often think that we need to put ourselves last, or that we need to suffer to make something happen. But that is not true! It is important to take time to do what makes you happy.

When you take time to do things that make you feel good, your entire perspective on life can change. You may find that by simply taking time to do something you enjoy – like reading a book, going for a walk, or having coffee with friends – your mood can shift dramatically. Taking time for yourself is just as important as taking care of others, and it is vital for maintaining a healthy lifestyle. It is not always easy to do what makes you happy. We

Renew

often let obligations get in the way of our happiness, which can lead to stress and fatigue. To help manage this, try making a list of things that bring you joy, and then try to do one of these activities each day. This will help you refocus your energy on what truly matters – living your best life.

When it is all said, and done, you are here to experience life in the most blissful way possible. It is your duty and obligation that you make all the things you desire to occur in your life. You are the source of your happiness. You are the peace of your heart. You are the key to unlocking your true potential. If you rely on a higher source, love yourself unconditionally, forgive others, and focus on nothing in this world can stop you doing anything. You are a diamond. You are limitless. Your energy will last forever. I love you and pray that whatever happens in your life is filled with abundance, love, and peace. Thank you again from the bottom of my heart for reading this book.

ABOUT THE AUTHOR

Rashad Young is a St. Louis native who currently resides in Chicago Illinois. He is an educator, counselor and Podcast Host of the Knowing is Knowing Podcast, and Speaker. What is important to Rashad is getting people to believe beyond their capabilities. With a promising future ahead, Rashad aspires to continue crafting stories that resonate with readers of all backgrounds.

Made in the USA
Monee, IL
28 December 2023